NUCLEAR FAMILY

THE HUGH MacLENNAN POETRY SERIES

Editors: Allan Hepburn and Carolyn Smart

TITLES IN THE SERIES

Nuclear Family

JEAN VAN LOON

McGill-Queen's University Press
Montreal & Kingston • London • Chicago

ISBN 978-0-2280-1115-6 (paper)
ISBN 978-0-2280-1355-6 (ePDF)
ISBN 978-0-2280-1356-3 (ePUB)

Legal deposit second quarter 2022
Bibliothèque nationale du Québec

Printed in Canada on acid-free paper that is 100% ancient forest free
(100% post-consumer recycled), processed chlorine free

We acknowledge the support of the Canada Council for the Arts.

Nous remercions le Conseil des arts du Canada de son soutien.

Library and Archives Canada Cataloguing in Publication

Title: Nuclear family / Jean Van Loon.

Names: Van Loon, Jean, author.

Series: Hugh MacLennan poetry series.

Description: Series statement: The Hugh MacLennan poetry series |
  Poems.

Identifiers: Canadiana (print) 20210393025 | Canadiana (ebook)
  20210393122 | ISBN 9780228011156 (softcover) |
  ISBN 9780228013556 (PDF) | ISBN 9780228013563 (ePUB)

Classification: LCC PS8643.A5495 N83 2022 | DDC C811/.6—dc23

This book was typeset by Marquis Interscript in 9.5/13 Sabon.

For Ian and Jamie Brown

CONTENTS

NUCLEAR FAMILY

HIROSHIMA, AFTER

No   sound

       sun

       shelter

       streetcars

No   family or other trees

No   wires to hurry words
       beyond the force field
       of loss

Few   humans stagger,
       blistered skin hanging
       from their limbs.

Says the White House
the greatest
achievement of organized science.

3

Says Leo Szilard
one of the greatest
blunders in history.

Otto Frisch sickens
as colleagues book
tables to celebrate.

Second Lieutenant Fussell, set
to invade an archipelago, knows
he can grow up after all.

        Of my father's response
        no record
        no living memory.

Bodies
fill the river
water invisible.

All the birds burned in flight.

A MAN OF FEW WORDS

It's all right to telephone the island that is a mirage.
It's all right to hear the gray voice.

Tomas Tranströmer

Phrases you used return –
Tinkerty-tonk as you left for work –
lines from verses I can't recall –
A barefoot boy with shoes on.

I am cells of your cells
bends of your brain, you who slipped
into sleep holding a tome
called *Porcelain*, who parried

my childish questions with *Get me
the Chemical Engineers' Handbook*,
wandered through it distracted
by questions I had not asked.

Your surname: Brown, like
your tweeds, and the wingtips
you sported in summer. You hosed
the car in a dress shirt – T-shirts

were for boys. The whole family giggled
at *Winnie the Pooh* and Ogden Nash,
P.G. Wodehouse and *Sarah Binks*.
You laughed out loud at Birney's

Turvey. Mum said it was *risqué*,
you only liked it because
of his prairie voice. No tales
of Auntie, her roses, her nursing

through World War One,
her brick house in Winnipeg.
Or of your father plying
highways for John Deere

in Depression Manitoba. When
Mum berated Dick
for his flawed piano recital, vetoed
our ice cream celebration

you said nothing. When daily
her tongue flensed Teddy
for something he could not help
your mouth firmed shut.

Days before you died
you gave each
a peck on the cheek.
I pushed away

your prickly chin. *A man
of few words*, your boss's
tribute. In photos, a seamed
smile. I cannot recall your voice.

But I keep listening

THEY CAME

From Winnipeg: your sister Rhoda,
        black-haired like you,
                but with eyes pale blue,

and her kind-faced husband Lory,

        faces Jane remembered
from the snowy Easter weekend they stayed with you,
                once in her fourteen years.

Your jolly brother Mel
        travelled from Winnipeg, too.

                Mel, who when business took you west,
greeted you at the railway station

        This is the bullet that shot the moose.

His plump wife Isabel,
                who hummed in nyloned feet
        as she fried a feast of chicken
in your unaccustomed kitchen

the time they camped their way east.
        Did it make you happy
                to have Mel near
        when you and he pitched tent in the afternoon
park, your three kids steeped
                in canvas-scented heat?

Claxton came, your bachelor brother-in-law –
                short
                big-bellied
                cigarette dribbling ash
telling stories,
                first to laugh at his jokes.
Who introduced you to Liz.

Florist's trucks came: heavy bouquets
                from neighbours and friends,
                        fellow workers
in the metallurgical lab,

                each array with a card
                        so tiny
                it held only printed wishes.

                Flowers,
            even from Lory and Rhoda,
                    their presence not enough,
the number of arrangements
                            a score,
            to show you'd been loved.

Platters of sandwiches came –
                salmon, chopped egg –
            peanut butter cookies,
            macaroni and cheese
            cold ham –
                packed into unstable stacks
                    around the kitchen,
            crammed into the fridge.

Mail came: pictures of flowers,
occasional angels. From your ancient aunts
in Winnipeg –
Aunt Selena, Aunt Lil – sisters
of the late Auntie,

who fed and guided you
after your mother died.
From Liz's
best friend, who gave Jane her middle name,
who married into the States. They came

through the cold spring suburb
to the house
you and Liz designed, built by your neighbour

across the street, his wife a former nurse,
one of the first
who bent where you lay
on the basement's concrete floor.

I don't like the angle of his neck, she said.
Angle created by Jane
in dimly recalled first aid,
when your air passages released a tortured snore.

Barely noticeable, red trickle from the small hole
in your temple.
Not far from your side
the metal tube none of them recognized,
protrusion at one end
to cradle your finger.

                    Lilies and roses came
            ferns and baby's breath.
They banked the living room,
                    blocked the fireplace,
                    covered the windowpane.

        Scent spread, leaden.

The donors arrived in solemn suits, offering
            deepest sympathy and a handshake.

                    Ole.
                    Bill.
                    Arvid.
                    Miss Doyle.

        Names Jane had heard
when you talked about work.
            Liz's friends and their husbands
                    companions for dinner and bridge

before Liz became misfit.

Wedgewood cups
                            rattled in saucers,
                    as the guests were rattled
even Jane could see.

            They came to see you
lying in polished mahogany
                    face to the coved ceiling
            that no longer gave you pleasure, the walls

of stylish cloudy-day grey buffered
        by blooms and polished shoes.

In the night, Jane comes by herself. Tiptoes
        down the stairs, feet bare,
                dim room empty

except for the flowers
        and you.
            With a single finger

she touches your cheek.

FUSION

Slender man, black-haired. Quiet
confidence. *Lovely to meet you*
says the young Ottawa woman.

Arnie's hazel eyes engage her blues.
From Winnipeg, a scientist.
Government lab. His voice

seeps through Liz, then and later.
She feels aligned when he's
beside her. Mere months

till a tiny diamond blinks
from her finger. Her Bank of Canada
fellows throw a farewell party.

In three years, VE celebrations
on Parliament Hill, near the Bank.
News photo of young women

in smart office suits, curls swinging
free. Her eye tarries there. Wriggling
Jane creases her fresh-pressed lap.

Open streetcar window – feeble
       surcease from the heat of people

summer-weight jacket
       limp on Arnie's forearm.

Damp sidewalk, each footstep
       a shock in his shoulders.

Ice cream brick from Boushey's
       melts as he climbs to the flat.

Jane, in the new dress Liz
       finished smocking last night,

speeds bare feet across the floor,
       tightens plump arms

around his knees.
       His breathing eases.

He was into the office early
       to hear the news in detail

not made public. Birth
       of the atomic bomb, christened

Gadget, its test Trinity, to be followed
       soon by two more children

          Little Boy, Fat Man

In the night her whitened toes
cold sole on his calf
between his palms he warms
a slender foot –
twig bones, taut skin.

Each day her mother phones.
Has that child been out? Steep
stairs from the second floor,
carriage ever heavier
back wheels roll the step-
edge, thunk onto the next
checked by her young back.

Downtown sidewalks
sometimes ploughed. North
winds down Elgin Street, raw-red
cheeks. She tucks the baby blanket
close. The numb in her heels
climbs. She pictures the wide
front hall of the mansion
she passes – fireplace, thick rug.

For Christmas he splurges.
On the swaying streetcar home
he hauls new overshoes lined
with lambswool, fleece flounce
at the calf and down the laced-up
front. Named after Winter Olympics
glossed by Hollywood. Boots
shaped like teakettles.

Years later, in icy wind
outside a rented house, Liz pegs
the wash, wearing Sun Valley boots
battered and scratched. Kicks them off
in the summer kitchen, next
to her husband's toe rubbers,
and brown galoshes
small, medium, large.

SAHTU LAKE

called by whites Great Bear

its five watery arms
span forest and tundra
embrace the Arctic Circle

sluggish fish
stick to their own
arm

Sahtu Dene
peer through woodsmoke
drying giant trout.

They track barrenland caribou
hunt moose in the muskeg
springtime geese and ducks

trap fox in the woodlands
gather berries and herbs
in the Scented Grass Hills.

By Deline village, lake-drain
breaks river ice. Men
fish cisco all year round.

A rock is a rock is

      solid as

    you're my

eternal.

On the lake's east shore
cool rock radiates

healing breath for tubercular lungs
glycerine-mix to smooth on cancers of the skin

salts drunk down in dosages
absorbed through baths. Radium

chemical symbol Ra
Sun King of Egypt.

Also in the lake's
steep eastern cliffs

              ore my father
              will purify for war

uranium 235
seven hundred million years

decaying. Each unstable nucleus
    sends out rays
        births daughters that send out more –
            alpha blocked by paper
                beta by a thin wood wall
                    gamma by thick lead sheet
            neutrons that pass through bodies

of miners lured by work
        and Sahtu bearers, pollened in radium dust
           hauling uranium ore on their backs
                in burlap sacks
            torn sacks borne home
   to mend the tents
      in the village of widows.

A ROCK IS A ROCK IS A ROCK

Quartz, Arnie says. Sandstone
from under a long-ago sea.
Mica in silvery slices.

Dick holds up stones
wherever he goes
asks their names.

Pitchblende pumps
particles into air, invisible
but for smears

on photo film
shadow on lungs
mushroom cloud.

NEW BROTHER

Chubby king rules
from his wooden throne
bangs his silver christening mug
on the highchair tray
if service is slow
or the food below snuff.

He stands sturdy-legged
at the front door screen
commands his big brother
to the back. Posed
for a photo, he's dwarfed
by an easy chair, legs crossed

brown ankle boots, a necklace
of fat wooden beads his royal
adornment. Dick and Jane
attend, one hand on the chair back
in the other a Sunwheat
biscuit, a Dinky Toy.

IPANA

Teddy hides behind Liz.
Dick, four years old, giggles
Daddy, Daddy. Home at last from a long
long trip, you spread before them
astonishing things – Ipana toothpaste

the kind you all use but tubed
in unusual colours; suitcase stickers
from South African Airways; tales
of the world's most beautiful climate,
too bad about the government.

Jane is seven, with the dimmest notion
of what you mean. You present her
with a plaid sundress she instantly loves.
Maroon, soft golds and greens. *Those
colours won't suit her*, says Liz.

You know better. Jane wears it whenever
the weather allows until it becomes
too small. A dress other girls envy
can't hope for,
with fathers always here.

Your letters flew home on Airmail
paper edged in red and blue. Was that
the trip you wrote it didn't matter
if you didn't come home:
Liz would have the insurance?

Yesterday Jane stopped at a store window:
a man's shirt, plaid,
in her dress's colours.
Her arms warmed
as on a childhood sundress day.

Ceilings high like church.
A hum from boxy machines
connected to pipes that stretch
and bend overhead, strapped tight
by steel bands bolted fast to plaster.
Might a pipe explode? Is that why
the wall clock is tucked inside a cage?
Do the valves with round red-rippled
grips turn the pipes safe?

Not the weekday father. No jacket, no tie.
He wanders from dial to dial
clipboard in hand, taking notes
whistling *Red River Valley*.

Side to side Jane's roller skate key
        slaps her chest, steel butterfly
on a long shoelace

        and she flies too, swoops past Coulter's
Drugs, wings a-swing
        with every four-wheeled stroke

ball-bearing smooth, looping
        her way through fedora'd fathers
burdened by briefcases

        and hunger. Fast and faster, grit
jitters her shins, face flashing
        past the glass of Sager's Shoes,

and the window with stacks of TVs
        on to The Bush, the scratchy
scrub where dangers lurk

        and girls especially must not go,
to Bank and Grove, End of the Line
        for streetcars and Jane. She unbuckles

the leather ankle strap, keys
        loose the grips for her shoes
and crosses The Bush to home.

She hears Arnie's briefcase click
         onto the floor. He slips his fedora
onto the cloakroom shelf.

She'll remember the daily click
         long after
she stops hearing it.

Chicago's Stagg Field, vacant
college football stadium. Below,
former squash courts. *This will do
for our Met Lab*, says Enrico Fermi.
The clock counts down.

Ottawa. Sunday afternoon yawns.
Sunday school done, other fun
shuttered. Arnie naps on Liz's
grey rug, forehead on lapped hands.

Black bricks stack to make a flattened
sphere, blocks of graphite unprecedented
for purity. One layer in three drilled
and uranium-filled. Neutron-absorbing
rods slot the walls.

Teddy craves a game, crawls
onto Arnie's back, wiggles, giggles. Excited,
Dick layers too, and I, though wary
of blast, venture atop the tower of totter.

Rods slide out, one by one. Each neutron
count matches Fermi's forecast. At last
a scientist draws the final rod, inch by measured
inch. Chain reaction. Sustained!
Chicago Pile goes critical.

The breathing mountain heaves
onto his side, and we explode
across the floor, propelled into hilarity.
Let's play Big Pile again.

Rods replaced, the chain shuts down,
Fermi's numbers accurate.
Fortunate, for the thousands
in surrounding shops
and homes.

KNUCKLEBONES

Carol Green and I
     and her sister Margaret Rose
          throw jacks on my front porch.

       Little metal stars.
    Margie scatters them
              too far.

      I slip them into a soft cloth bag
         tuck in the ball
         tighten the strings

     and we're off
          to Greens' house three doors down
  for lunch.

Front room blind
      drawn. Mr Green at home.

          Dim inside.

    He lies on the chesterfield
      feet hanging from one of the arms.

He inspects fires,
      pokes through ruins, finds

        what made flame start.

From a chair pulled close Mrs Green whispers
make yourselves a sandwich.

Dry. Peanut butter. Carol mashes it with Miracle Whip.
We pour ourselves milk
talk   quietly
like Mrs Green.

Mr Green's shoulders fill the doorway.

His fireman's eyes,
that stared blue bullets
the day I slapped Margie

dark
rimmed with red.

Cinders,
he says.

Couldn't even tell they were children.

FISSION

A spill of India ink –
terror blots Europe
expels
        Teller
          Szilard
            Fermi
              Frisch
                Franck

highly charged minds impelled
to nuclei of science
in Berkeley   Chicago

Oak Ridge   Los Alamos.
      Ideas   orbit
around an urgent need.

Radioactive ores migrate
to New Mexico desert

  from Congo through Staten Island
    from Colorado mines

      from Great Bear Lake
          via Port Hope and the Ottawa labs

              where my young father
              stretches metallurgy
              to wrest the most from ores.

Physics chemistry mathematics   rock
bombarded by US dollars
achieve critical mass –

Hiroshima.
          Nagasaki.
Fallout

taints vast tracts
sea and land
                    and my father's desk.

DRILL

The heat
         would burn you up
                  the light
blind

         that's why

when the warning wail climbs like a fire reel's siren
         holding then and holding through our ears
                           and arms and bellies
                  then slides way down
                  like someone crying
         from the metal megaphone
                  on the high post on Bank Street
                           near the bridge

         dive under desks
         eyes tight
                  and cover them
                  with crossed arms.

Can my arm
         save my eyes?
Sneak a look?

Who else is peeking?

Echoes shiver

         in my skin.

1966. The TV mystery man wears
a pillowcase, eyes and mouth cut
in zeroes, accented speech like code.

September 1945. Igor Gouzenko
slips through the empty
Soviet Embassy. Crams a briefcase

with codebooks and ciphered signals:
evidence of western defences
gnawed by Red Army moles.

109 files. Two leather straps
latch the satchel closed.
He locks the door

on pay cheque and homeland, steps
            into void.
His files will buy asylum.

He spreads covert messages on a desk
at *The Ottawa Journal*. On behalf
of readers, the night editor yawns.

In the Justice Department lobby
the white-haired commissionaire shrugs,
they're all home asleep.

Prime Minister King's closest advisors
hurry advice to Laurier House. In slippers
King replies, *Stalin's our ally*.

A neighbour scoops Gouzenkos into his flat
across the hall from their own. Outside
on Somerset Street, black sedans creep to a stop.

Gouzenko squints through the keyhole. Heavy
Soviet oxfords tread the brown linoleum
to his door. It splinters open.

RCMP intelligence decodes
Gouzenko's cache, transmits him
and family to Camp X.

In Canada, the US, Britain
secret-sworn eyes
widen.

Somewhere in a small
Ontario town, a Mr Brown
moves in.

CROWNED

Honey-coloured mucilage oozes
        from the slant of the bottle's rubber nipple
onto the back of a *Citizen* photo

        for Jane's scrapbook. The page puckers
under Princess Elizabeth and Princess Margaret Rose,
        with their Corgis. *Who's ever seen a Corgi?*

TV brings home Westminster Abbey full of the chosen.
        The Archbishop of Canterbury
white-haired, in weighty robe, dips

        a finger in holy oil, Princess Elizabeth
hidden beneath an embroidered canopy, and Oh –
        strange feeling in Jane's private parts –

he reaches beneath the silken screen, touches
        Elizabeth's breast
anoints her

        Queen.

PLUNDER

The summer morning opens like a story
    school-free weeks
        friends away for holidays.

On the bottom step of the porch
    I snap twigs into pieces
        long for a nickel to buy a Tootsie Roll.

Up Bank Street past the corner store –
    shelves of blackballs, BB Bats and bubblegum –
        past Hill's Taxi, Sager's Shoes

to the schoolyard, empty as a yawn.
    I penetrate the Boys' Yard – foreign ground
        packed by alien feet – drawn

to a bar-rimmed window well. I scale the rust-roughed pipe
    leap into the concrete fortress, crouch
        unseen. My hands smell of blood.

Everything
is in the hands
of God, says Juda

king of no one
of any account
as the tests begin

on his kingdom
Bikini Atoll
after Hiroshima and Nagasaki.

          My father and mother study house plans
          from Central Mortgage and Housing.
          They buy a treed lot, spread blueprints.

Sixty-seven tests:
Castle Bravo alone
a thousand Hiroshimas.

The no ones are moved
from atoll to atoll
to escape radiation

each new situation
smaller, with less food
and water

until at last
in the care of the US Navy
they starve.

Beds, the drop-leaf dining table
    Liz and Arnie bought
when they married, the old upright piano
    from Arnie's family, the yellow arborite
where they ate in the old-house kitchen –

muscled magicians float them up a ramp,
    2 x 8s that promise stairs
to the front stoop. Like stucco promised to cover
    the metal mesh on the second storey,
curbs and pavement for the street

storm sewers to replace the deep ditches
    singing with crickets.
Banished from the adults' harried turf, Jane tramps
    the yard's rough dirt, tree-shadowed
and planted with building debris.

Behind it the spring-quick creek
    deep enough to spill into Jane's boots.
Minnows, small green frogs too fast to catch,
    spotted orange flowers with tender stems
that break when she brushes past.

Behind all that, two shacks clad
    in Insulbrick. Rooster-crow, chicken-clucks
woods with a wildflower she's never seen before,
    Dutchman's Breeches, white pantaloons
hung from a bending stem.

Outside her room's wide window
        a basswood tree. Its windy leaves
swim like lily pads. Through darkening
        green, a growing moon
winks.

FALLOUT (*ii*)

In France's post-war
freedom, people throng
the beaches.

Fabric scarce, a bold
designer tests
a new bathing suit:

three triangles in front,
two up, one down, and one
behind, linked by strings.

It must be small enough,
to pass
through a wedding ring.

        My father travels to parties
        that launch uranium mines.
        Australia, South Africa,

        The Canadian north. Atomic
        power will fuel
        the future.

        In Ottawa, after lab-work,
        he sleeps in his easy chair.
        After dinner, dozes.

At the dining table, you hold the naked
wooden spool in your pipe-yellow fingers.
The boys and I lean into your smoky

aura to watch your pocketknife notch
a slot across one end, flick off the red tip
of an Eddy Strike-Anywhere match.

You snap a piece of the matchstick
to fit the slot, not beyond, slip
a thick elastic around it and through

the spool's centre. At the other end
you loop a longer shaft, turn
the long arm round and round

till the rubber tugs both sticks tight.
Set on the table, the spool rolls
like a tractor, long arm a plow.

A small strange journey out of
your far-away youth. We stare
rapt until the elastic slackens.

You and the boys tire of it.
I rewind the elastic,
twisting your boyhood close.

In the polish of your briar pipe. In cement
that secures bone handle to carving knife.
Gloss for Gobstoppers, Smarties, Mum's
headache pills. In Simoniz, final coat
for the still-new Buick, hand-washed

rubbed to gleam by you and the boys. (*Simoniz
your watches*, tired joke you never tire of).
Thickener in Jane's first lipstick, from Zellers
at Billings Bridge (Tangee Natural – orange
when worn, waxy aroma of adulthood).

Annual treatment of oak strip floors, the hottest
day of summer, Liz and Jane stripped to shorts
to strip old wax, rugs rolled and dragged
with table and chairs. Floor turpentine-soaked
section by section. Rags, steel wool, tough scrubs.

And now: Carnauba. Regal in shining steel.
Cloaked hands claw out emollience,
balm for finger pads. Royal aura
clouds the oak, summer-breeze dried
for the buffer's weighty attentions.

After it all, mellow:
floor-shine, house-scent
cool-bathed bodies
iced tea in slow sleek sips.

Russia's first atomic bomb
    blasts a secret steppe in Kazakhstan.

    Unsettling tremors trigger Western sensors.

Americans test one bigger.

Soviets another. Then the British. And the French.

Charnel dust rides winds that wrap the earth

               seeds clouds with radiant rain, Trojan gift
    to tallgrass prairies and living rivers

                   rinse
    of invisible light that seeps
        into skin and marrow
            and like strong drink
                eats us from inside.

It melts into the milk
    of Arctic mothers
        their toddlers' teeth

powders hot city pavements
    collects in unswept corners of cheap rooms

unsettles us –

earthquake we can't quite sense

torn dream that hangs dark over morning

news we wish we did not know

treasure we can't remember but know we've lost.

It settles like fear
                   into our language

bomb shelter   *Doomsday Clock*   *Missile Gap*

TITLES

Director, Commercial Products Division
Atomic Energy of Canada Limited

Shirley's dad sells bombs to the Russkies, he says,
                              cobalt bombs.

He tells her how long it takes to fly to the Soviet Union
                    how much vodka you have to drink
                              to make a sale,
                         how to use the listening devices
                    in your hotel
          to trick them into buying the higher-priced model.

Chief, Radioactivity Division
Department of Mines and Technical Surveys

Jane's father brings home a Geiger counter –
               brisk ticks over the watch
                         with the luminous dial
                              over the Lucite penholder
          from the opening of Gunnar Mine
                    yellowcake and a dark lump
          of pitchblende.

                    ticks over the Fiesta dinnerware
                         navy   green   yellow.

At the orange plate Jane's mother uses

          rat-a-tat-tat static.

New uranium mines dot maps
of Australia, South Africa,
northern Saskatchewan

even here in Ontario.
Dad flies to the mines,
knows their men,

and the men feast
at our dining room table,
Mum rosy, Dad leaning

in. My brothers and I
linger after the meal,
digesting the faces

the stories and jokes,
the way Australians
say *die* for *day*.

We like them best –
their accents, their animals,
their birds. Even their mines

have lively names –
Mary Kathleen, Rum Jungle.
One man has a daughter

Gwenda. I post her
a sketch of our cute squirrel.
She mails me koala photos

writes in clear square script
that looks like printing
about her "grammar school."

Her biology textbook fills
our mailbox: grey, thick, hard-
covered. Startling chapter

on rabbit reproduction. People
must do these things too.
Why would they want to?

I think of young Queen Elizabeth
and her duke. Her duty
to bear a royal heir.

Oh whence for me
shall my salvation come.
Hymn 842 in the United Church
hymnbook. Listed on the newsprint
sandwich board on the school
gym's stage.
     The folding wooden
chairs make Jane squirm. She stares
at Mrs Beatty's flop-brimmed
hat, Mrs McLean's ocelot
turban and pearly teardrop
earring. Her father, an elder,
passes the plate for collection.

Dr Murdstone fulminates –
her mother's word –
today about recorded music,
mistakes erased. Glenn Gould
can tell it's fraud, Dr Murdstone says,
God can tell. Movies are not evil,
he says, just silly. Rock and roll
is not evil, just silly.
Science is evil.

He drapes himself over the pulpit
black robes spread
like the wings of a merciless bird.
Red face, bald pate pulsing:
scientists
are leading us all to hell.

FALLOUT (*iii*)

Twenty-three fishermen chase tuna
in a South Pacific zone
outside US restrictions.

They watch sun rise
in the west, catch
ash, grey snow in their hands.

The half-life of the crew:
ninety minutes.
Survivors die slowly

years-long torture,
skin tormented,
their newborns twisted.

It's unreasonable,
says Edward Teller,
to make such a big deal

over the death
of a fisherman.

> In 1958 on a woodsy street
> in a new Ottawa suburb,
> in a house my parents designed,

my father –
a bit of a pacifist
my mother later explains –

rises one morning and
detonates his brain.

VERGE

The world verges on turning
night to day, swollen buds
to leaves, soiled remains of winter
into summer's softened earth. It slows

for this moment, verges on crushing
assumptions into rubble. Crouched
by the vent, hurrying for school, I
dry my hair in the furnace's warm air.

Mum plumps the eiderdown,
tilts venetian slats, admits emerging
morning. Thursday once again.
One footstep follows another.

Teddy rises from submerged
splashes in his bath, clean
clothes laid out for a cool-guy
swagger to Grade 5.

Shirt mostly tucked, Dick
searches for his socks, dreaming
magma seethes below rock's surface
ready to flame the shoots of May.

Still the moment.
As long as we stay upstairs
we do not know
our world has lurched.

Dad? Dick at four follows our father,
yellow power shovel held to his hip, striped
t-shirt stretched to fit over his head, follows
him into the dark garage with the leaf rakes
and rusty reel-style mower that sounds "swish"
with every push. *Dad?* follows Dad.

Aged eleven Dick tracks Dad
into the garage of the new house –
paved floor, straight walls, a gasoline mower
for big lawns front and back. Dad
shows how: pull till it catches,
turn back the choke.

School-day morning. Dick hears
a bang downstairs, where Dad has gone
to start the coffee. I hear it too,
call down, *What did you drop?* My
snarky voice. No answer.
Dad must be fuming.

Dick laces his Sisman Scampers. He'll
need new ones for summer camp. He calls
down the stairs, *Dad* – into the kitchen
where breakfast should be, *Dad* –
down to the basement.
Dad? Dad!

COLD COMFORT

Under the landing,
in the basement's dim back corner
a chair from the old house.
Chrome legs rubber-footed

blotched. Round steel seat
dipped in the middle, back
a metal rectangle. Chipped
paint, layers of colour.

Why was it kept for the new house?
Who chose the sunny yellow?
Jane has sat in it for over-broiled
pork chops and grey canned peas.

A neighbour draws it near Liz.
The doctor rises from beside
the shape on the floor, says
to Liz something Jane cannot hear.

Liz's hands spread over her face.
Oh no, she says, and sits
on cold hard steel.

aftershocks

mum on the basement chair
    face buried in her hands

        the concrete under my feet
    craters   beside my father's body

the doctor snaps his black bag
    shut   someone suggests I go upstairs

the coffee dad started explodes
    into the perk's glass peak

        between one moment and the next
between breath and no breath –

        breadth of a baby's hair
            smallest particle of an instant

everything

who'll be our face to the world?
who will protect us from mum?

will we be poor? have to move?
    what was that long metal tube on the floor?

from the brown box dad brought home
with the mother's day chocolates?

in the back yard two men in suits
tug cedar hedge branches aside
searching   for something

        a reason

WHAT THE NEW WIDOW TELLS
HER NINE-YEAR-OLD SON

He sits in his bath:
bed wet
again.

Poisoned air each morning
stench of ammonia
and the sound of her voice

denouncing his moral failure –
he'll never go to camp
never get married –

her tongue honing its edge
on each new dawn.
After the doctor has confirmed

the worst, she climbs from the basement
dizzy – her scolding
the last words her husband heard.

She pounds
the boy's naked shoulders,
This is all your fault.

WHAT THE NEW WIDOW TELLS
HER ELEVEN-YEAR-OLD SON

He doesn't know.
His green eyes translate
from what she's saying
to sun on his skin,
river spill, prick of gills,
smell of earthworms and perch,
coming weekend for him and Dad
with a friend and his father
if he had remembered
to mention the invitation.

Whatever she says, he hears
if only.

How lovely the flowers from my uncle's friend Don,
best man for my parents' wedding. How thoughtful

the bouquets from Dad's office, the curling club,
the United Church ladies, our neighbours, Mum's faraway

childhood friends. How handy the platter of sandwiches
Shirley's mother made. How to ledge

another casserole on the fridge's stacked
shelves. When the body will return

from Hulse and Playfair Funeral Home to rest
in the living room. How long it will take us

to eat all these cakes and cookies and squares.
How important to write thanks

for even the briefest of sympathy cards. Whether
I will sleep in Dad's twin bed

so Mum's Aunt Garnie, experienced
widow, can use my room for a while.

Who will iron the pillowslips, mow the lawn,
vacuum the drapes, after Mum finds a job.

How she will dress for work, safety-pin a pleat
in the waistband of her good tweed skirt,

newly inches too big. Even decades
later, I do not say that the flowers

reeked, that I hated the ways
their scent invaded, or how

for years I could not step
into a florist shop.

THE PERFUMED HOUSE

The scent of lilies –
thickest in the living
room where no-one
lives but a glossy box
presides, lined with satin.

Lying motionless, a form
in Dad's good suit. His high
forehead, his moustache.
His shaming yellow teeth
hidden behind closed lips.

Folded on his chest, hands
that showed me how to whittle
a whistle from spring willow.
Quick fingers that played piano
without a page of notes.

All still in this dim room
in the sleeping house. I tiptoe
close, wonder if his skin feels cold.
This is my father.
This is not my father.

On the day of the funeral Liz hustles the boys
        to play at a friend's.

She asks if Jane would like to go to the service. Jane's fourteen.
        It's the first warm day of spring.

She and a friend scuff across dead grass on a vacant lot.
        They toss a tattered softball, softly talking.

At funerals you learn things you wish you'd known before.
        Jane didn't know that then.

Later Liz recounts the procession to the cemetery,
        the stranger on the sidewalk who tipped his hat.

Jane pictures the casket sunk in a Beechwood knoll.
        Open wound

                of earth.
Permissible tears.

CHINESE FOOD

Home from the Ho Ho Café
with Shirley

and her family, the Mercury long
and low as seen on Ed Sullivan

gears that change
at a chrome button's click.

Jane steps from the car, tongue
sweet from pineapple chicken

flush-cheeked from Chinese tea
lips soy-saucy, laughing.

Sorry for your loss
says the girl across the street

face somber. Jane's laugh cuts
short   frozen

        between the car
where nothing has changed

and the house
where nothing's the same.

A KINDNESS

Jane's head jerks out of a doze. Evergreens
        blur past the window. The Mercury
murmurs. Her eyelids slump.

        Lunchtime, calls Shirley's mother
from the suicide seat. Jane and Shirley
        blink into noonday. Sun fades.

Asphalt unfolds. Shirley's mother
        doles another Gravol. Yesterday: giggles
all afternoon, Shirley's parents begging

        enough. Jane forgot about home. Knee deep
wade through rain-chilled grass. The Tidal
        Bore: gulls stab for tide-borne trash.

In motel dark, Jane wonders what she'll find
        at home. What more gone wrong.
In Halifax, the tide is out. All mud.

        With fresh seafood sandwiches, they wander
unposted roads seeking an oceanside picnic.
        Windows down, they follow gull cries

to a dump sparkling with glass and cans,
        aflap with screaming birds. Shirley's parents
chuckle, and unwrap the waxed paper.

Awake in the night, Jane pictures a speeding car
cresting a hill into the windshield
       another dark box in the living room.

Next day she races for the seat away
       from the highway centre. She clutches
the padded armrest all the long way home.

At the dark wood desk in the bedroom
Liz marshals her armoury – degree,
wartime work, the way she wrangles
the written word. Job a necessity now,

not unwelcome. Her husband's
fountain pen. Wine-red with a wide
gold band, trustworthy weight
in the hand. She tests it for flow

on the edge of her edited draft. No
blots for the final creamy paper. Date.
Is it only three months since he died?
Each day freighted. Return address.

Already drafted at this desk, *I-regret-
to-inform you* missives to Ottawa Hydro,
to the Canadian Institute of Mining
and Metallurgy, the curling club.

*Thank-you-sincerely-for-your-kind-
condolences* notes. The stack of cards
unanswered has shrunk to three.
This letter matters. *Dear Sir*:

After church she refrained
from complaint. An acquaintance
from the congregation invited her to write.
Department of Insurance. Sounds drab.

Does she have to actually write *sole*
breadwinner for a family of four? No.
This addressee knows. Any offer
likely to be Clerk Grade 1. Low pay.

But a foot in the door. No more listening
for the slip of mail through the slot,
the flop of disappointment on the floor.
Degree out of date. Stale experience.

The invisible shield she must pierce
sixteen years after the Bank of Canada:
the women of her graduating class
consigned to filing, men enlisted as analysts.

When he replies, she'll buy a large carton
of ice cream in chocolate, vanilla,
strawberry. The kids will trickle home
hungry. She'll hold up his letter. Bent

at the folds, it'll wave like a sail
in the breeze from a window
open to golden fall. *Dear Sir:*
she'll write. *I am pleased to accept …*

Much of this may not
be fact. Jane does remember
returning from rummy with friends

her mother in the driveway
face full of sun, saying
I have a job.

Down the basement stairs
Liz and Jane at bedtime

flashlights in hand for the shadow
behind the furnace, where bad guys
may lurk,

        they laugh,
as if they don't believe it.

Nights before Arnie's absence
turned normal.

A freezing wall
snaps, something scratches
the windowpane. Liz listens

for Jane, late home, wonders
how Dick
could lose new shoes.

Her bedside lamp
glows into empty hours,

her company the streetlight.

Night rain slow on the sill
        drop   drop   a knell.
Bedsheets wintry
        and her abandoned feet.

TV mystery she turned off –
        fatherless boy, gang's deft stealth,
his test a knife drawn deep,
        opened throat.   Here, two

fatherless boys under a roof
        she alone holds up. Its weight:
wet laundry hauled upstairs
        weary feet in winter boots.

Daughter a butterfly fluttering
        low over ravenous swamp
fresh flesh in a jungle of probing
        tongues, persistent paws.

Rain-drums echo the drunk
        from the curling club bar, knuckles
that pummeled front door oak
        for her undefended self.

She tosses in cotton tangle
        casts an arm out
for anchor, for the hand
        no longer there.

Outside it's cold, but in the dark car
dashboard glow, scent of fried onion
from takeout burgers after the dance.

They feast while looking out
at the river rippling light
from the bridge. Words and silences

weave a thickening mesh
between Jane and this tall classmate
with the handsome profile

she keeps glancing at, and a grip
that scallops the steering wheel
when he drives. Time ticks.

Back home, she fumbles the door key
fifteen minutes after curfew's curtain.
Upstairs, her mother's slippers slap:
slut, slut, slut.

Before breakfast, Liz and Jane
       yawn their way downtown. Saturday streets
windswept. Empty. Ballroom after the ball.

In the oily dim of Cabeldu's
       service bay, white-coated Mr Mason
clipboard-lists the Buick's afflictions.

Jane and Liz hustle, fall coats hugged close,
       to the Honey Dew Café's cinnamon warmth.
Dunked sweet buns. Infinite coffee refills

until the stores are open. Swinging strides
       to Sparks Street. They tug Morgan's weighty door
against the wind, test scents – *Chanel*

and *Joy* – and ride the brass cage up
       to ladies' wear. Cruising the racks, they stroke
silken folds. Across the street in Birks, diamonds

in glass cases spark fancies. In thick
       Green Dragon incense they trail glittering
trinkets across their wrists. The final stop

Murphy-Gamble's bakery – line-up
       for sugar-crust muffins and warm
white loaves. Home they roll,

wreathed in yeast. Teddy scowls
          by the door, fists plunged
into his windbreaker. The cat beside him glares.

Where were you? says Teddy. Tigger
          plants fangs in Jane's ankle. Laden with grace,
Liz laughs and unlocks the door.

Summer streams through open windows
'59 Falcon lent by Dougie's dad
my lilac-shampooed hair blows wild
seven of us in seats for five

fresh-pressed smell of summer cottons
young limbs hot against others
my boyfriend's femurs a hard seat
but fine with me. We speed

along unknown roads, churning
a wake of dust, lost, retracing,
lost again, in quest of still-raw
lakefront soon to become a park.

After lunch on sun-patched blanket
lumped by rock and root
our leavings – orange peel, paper cups
half an egg-salad sandwich.

Water beads on skin cooled
by pristine swim. Beer cans
tilt, laughs peal heedless
until a shout –

      a placid black-rope coil
      wraps a warming boulder

We girls stand distant, towel shawled.
Boys ring round him, armed with deadfall
clubs. Thuds. Old dozer stirs. Shrugs.
He whips and lashes. Stops.

      how many years has he grown here
      amid wintergreen, birch, and spruce

      to reach six feet
      blacken his youthful blotches

Our chatter subsides for a while
rises again less fresh, less free.
We are older than we were.

Gathering blanket, hampers, trash
we leave the dusk-tinted lake,
its edges shimmering
              hundreds of little snakes.

GOTTA GET OUT OF THIS PLACE /
CAN'T GET NO ...

1 Br. Central pops
from the *Citizen* want-ads.
Sunny. Hdwd. 1 bth.

Jane will paint the walls cream
sew yellow curtains for a window
into a worldly street,

walk to her office, cook
for her friends. Evenings out
without thought of clock.

She'll buy a braided rug
bring her bed, the bookcase
with glass doors ...

       Her mother's shadow
darkens the page. *That's right.*
Take all you can get

then leave.

The sports car shines from the dealer's lot
like a parked sun. '68 Firebird Sprint.
Liz's fifty-year-old heart rises
from the rust flakes of her faded Buick Special.

GM calls the paint "Goldenrod"
but that's an August name. She
sees April daffodil, May dandelion
the jubilant June hue of a circus train.

She doesn't care about zero to sixty
or the engine – DeLorean's pride –
loves how the Firebird crouches for flight
while standing in the drive.
She flies to her government job,

to grocery store, curling club, home.
The mileage mounts, inches
at a time. Years fly with her,
taints of dried-blood rust
instantly stanched by the dealer's styptic.

Intent young men at the hi-test fill-up
offer cash, lusting
for overhead cams and the four-barrelled
carburetor, the Firestone wide ovals
ringed by a thin red line.

From the snug white bucket seat of naugahyde
　　she grips the shiny floor-mount shift
　　　　her tweeds transfigured to leather
　　　　　　wool scarf to rippling silk –
　from widowed mother to bachelor girl.

LEARNING YOU, DAD,
FROM THE WRONG END OF TIME

Cardboard frame, one corner blunted.
Jumbled among other photos
in the drawer of a disused dresser
inside a closet rarely opened –

you are almost twenty-two
on a survey crew up north
squinting in black and white
into pale arctic sun.

You stand with a fellow surveyor
geologist's hammer in hand –
perhaps to show the scale of happiness?
Shirt open, torn trousers

trailing like capes behind legs
bared from the knee. Bucket hat
battered. On your face – in this image
alone of all the ones I've seen –

a big true smile.

"Neat" was Mum's mantra.
Beds made before breakfast,
no feet, no cats on the furniture.
No newspapers on the sofa

or even the rug – ink might rub.
Spills cleaned in the moment.
Doorframes dusted. Curtains
vacuumed – one third weekly.

The camping you loved
must have been beyond
her imagining. You chose
a permanent escape.

After you died, I slept in your
twin bed to keep Mum company.
She cried at night, once pondered
if she should have married Bob –

who gave her an evening purse
made of antelope suede
his likeness close at hand
in her dressing table drawer

with her perfumes and pearls
and her face-powder music box.
He and she: blown hair,
easy smiles, loose-linked fingers.

Perhaps it was better,
I said, to have had you
a shorter time, than
a lesser man for longer.

When I was a child
I spake as a child.
When she died, decades later,
I kept the purse.

Tell me about when you fished
      with your friend and his father,
sodden sandwiches lined up to dry
      on the car trunk's edge. And the bear.

Tell me about the yellow morning,
      map in hand, finger tracing your plan,
three friends on bikes, back roads
      among alfalfa fields.

Tell me about the chilly river
      at the city beach, swimming,
cowlick dripping, your skin
      dappling blue.

Meccano pieces that clicked
      into hinges bound by a narrow rod,
the oily smell of the steam engine
      you begged for at Christmas.

Let me remember you
      young, in the kitchen,
flour-drifts across your jersey
      milk-ponds on the floor

window lighting your face,
      I'm making muffins. Like
the time Mum was in hospital
      and Dad baked apple pie.

Apron-wrapped, he lifted
        the phone, floured hand
on black receiver. He turned,
        You have a new brother.

Our tines raked burnished lines – rooms
imagined, gaps for doors, pictured
windows – until we kicked

the leaf-house to oblivion, pitched
the bits into bushel baskets, a nickel
apiece, upturned onto the pile

Dad heaped for burning. We leaped
into their damp sweet smell, leaf-mould
returning them to earth.

Leaves fall at their peak glory
as we hope we may do – but no –
who wants to leave when all is well?

Wouldn't we rather wither, suspended
from our stems, clinging
as long as we can?

First fall Dad was gone, we drove into
the Gatineau hills. Sun-crisped crimsons
quivered in the wind.

Below the lookout – hollow valley
diminished river, Dad's garden
entombed in unraked leaves.

In my former bedroom, Mum and I
sip tea. Outside, snow-dust spangles
from basswood limbs.

She snuggles into a love seat
lush in jungle-green chintz
beside a stepped bookcase

of white faux bamboo. Books press
shoulder to shoulder. Matching
novel covers parade along one shelf.

"*A Dance to the Music of Time,*"
she says. *My friends and I read them all.*
And there's the Proust of her first

retirement summer. *I thought every
educated person should have read it.*
Near the floor, proud of the shelf,

three spines I kneel to read –
Russian Cyrillic. *Oh those.*
I had to learn Russian for work.

Every workday, gatehouse guards
screened her through razor-wire,
sworn to say only, *I write reports.*

We is such a lovely word,
you said in hospice.
You who spoke it seldom
once your children had grown.

Solitaire by TV glow.
Books in piles, from library
or friends, but no warming chat
with milk in the bedtime kitchen.

"She had a bad night," the nurse
told me, "kept repeating *I'm
so so sorry.*" Final hospital stay
before hospice, roommate

howling *No* to invisible
priests and devils. How could I
probe your sorrow, you deaf,
roommate's family bulging

the pale fall of fabric between?
How could you confide, you
who shrouded sorrows, sealed
regrets in secret shame? *We*

is such a lovely word,
you told me, the last time
you sat up in bed. Sowing
a stone in my heart's folds.

Tenderly
    you held tiny toads
        in your little-boy fingers.

        You woke from a dream –
            cradling
    a fallen nest of baby birds.

You obeyed our mother
                muttered
            your disagreements
    watched her
        wary.

    You smashed a window at school
        with an India Rubber ball
            the principal had banned
                the previous day.

        Hockey stick wielded as weapon
            you cleared older boys from the pond
            you and your chums
                had cleared of snow.

    In high school, opposing football coaches
        warned their teams
                of you.

Last to leave home
      you sat with her evenings
            in the family room over the garage:
               Have Gun – Will Travel.
You helped stow groceries, shovelled snow
               mowed.

In her old age, when she no longer drove
             downtown
     you braved a winter highway to the city
        for Christmas shopping:
               Fisher's Menswear, Birks Jewellery.

               You treated her to lunch
         in carpeted quiet
      among white-haired diners.

The last week in hospice you kept her company
      day after day
         in the cramped silence
            beside her narrow bed.

      You worried about her grave
   cold in September rain.

Not long ago, you and I and Dick
      talked about the bang we heard that day.
        All of us remembered
           the exact words Dick shouted
      from the basement.

After sixty years.

     Only then
        did your rage

detonate.

The record I uncover among your northern photos
bears no label. It's 45-sized, but with a 78's

pencil-wide hole. Converted to CD, its strains
waver: *The West, a Nest* … Did you record it

from some lonely radio? Did you waltz to it
back home with Mum? She kept it till she died.

I can hardly decipher the sounds. Like the signal
from an AM station just out of reach.

FROM PORT RADIUM

Uranium ore travels
through World War Two
and beyond   Sahtu men

haul sacks of "money-rock"
onto the *Radium Gilbert*
to cross Great Bear Lake

      trailing grains

floating downriver they smoke
and sleep on the sacks   barge
with ore up the Mackenzie

      coating portages

Wrigley Fort Simpson Axe Point
Great Slave Lake

      dusting docks

Fort Smith   Fort Chipewyan
Lake Athabasca   to Waterways

      trickling the grail.

Railhead onward, steel
wheels roll heavy metal
to Port Hope's refinery

        ore-dust trail   1,500 miles
        each grain
        sparks particles
                like shooting stars

hundreds of millions of years

NOTES AND ACKNOWLEDGMENTS

Epigraph credit for "A Man of Few Words": Tomas Tranströmer, excerpt from "After a Long Dry Spell," translated by Robert Bly, from *The Half-Finished Heaven: The Best Poems of Tomas Tranströmer*. Copyright © 2001 by Tomas Tranströmer. Translation copyright © 2001 by Robert Bly. Reprinted with the permission of The Permissions Company, LLC, on behalf of Graywolf Press, graywolfpress.org.

My thanks to Tim Lilburn and my Sage Hill Spring Colloquium colleagues of 2017, whose inspirational companionship refined my gauzy imaginings into a critical mass. In Ottawa, the Sawdust Reading Series gave me a chance to test poems before an audience. Advice from my weekly Ruby Tuesday poetry group bombarded poetic nuclei to bring them closer to fissile state.

When I had lost momentum, Frances Boyle picked me up and pointed me in the right direction. Claudia Coutu Radmore's suggestion helped me couple the two strands of the book. David O'Meara generously advised on an early draft of the manuscript; the focus that he suggested for revision helped immensely. My husband Rick evolved from a non-reader of poetry to an astute and sometimes inspired editor.

Versions of some poems previously appeared in
Canadian periodicals: "Turning Leaves" and "Eden"
in *Arc*; "Carnauba, Queen of Waxes" in *Queen's
Quarterly*; "Peopling the Night" in *The Fiddlehead*;
and "Plunder" in *Glebe Report*. My thanks to the editors
of these publications.

An invaluable source for the Manhattan Project was
Richard Rhodes, *The Making of the Atomic Bomb*
(New York: Simon & Schuster, 1986).

Thank you to Allan Hepburn and Carolyn Smart of
McGill-Queen's University Press for seeing merit in
this work. With light-handed encouragement, and a subtle
eye and ear, Allan helped me bring out the best in it.
David Drummond created the perfect cover.

My deep gratitude to Ian and Jamie Brown for supporting
this enterprise despite the painful memories it evoked,
and most of all for being loving brothers.